Sounds in the House
Sonidos en la casa

A Mystery

BANG!

CLACK!

CREEK!

By Karl Beckstrand
Illustrated by Channing Jones

Sounds in the House! Sonidos en la casa: A Mystery

Premio Publishing & Gozo Books
Midvale, UT, USA
ISBN: 978-0985398873

Text Copyright © 2011 Karl Beckstrand
Illustrations Copyright © 2011 Channing Jones
ebook ISBN: 978-1452411408

Available in English, Spanish, and ebook versions / Pida este libro en inglés, Español o como ebook: **PremioBooks.com**

Spanish vowels have one sound each: a = ah e = eh i = ee o = oh u = oo.
Every vowel should be pronounced (except for the *u* after a *q* [que is pronounced keh]). In Spanish, the letter *j* is pronounced as an English *h* (and the letter *h* is silent), *ll* sounds like a *y* (or a **j** in some countries), and *ñ* has an ny sound (año sounds like ah-nyo).

Spanish nouns are masculine or feminine and are usually preceded by an article: *la* = feminine *the*; *el* = masculine *the*; *una* = feminine *a* or *one*; *un* = masculine *a* or *one*. Articles (and **-s**/*-es* after nouns) reflect plural: *las* = plural feminine *the*; *los* = plural masculine *the*; *unas* = feminine *some*; *unos* = masculine *some*.

Las combinaciones de letras en inglés pueden cambiar los sonidos por completo: *ck* se pronuncia como *k; wr* se pronuncia como *r; ee* se pronuncia *i; qu* se pronuncia *cu; ai* se pronuncia *ey; ll* se pronuncia *l;* y *gh* no tiene sonido en medio, y al final, de la mayoría de las palabras. El sonido de ch (de chico) se ocupa al comenzar palabras, en el medio, y al final también.

Los sustantivos en inglés no tienen género; se usa *the* para *la, el, las,* y *los.* Algunas palabras en inglés — a pesar de escribirse de forma diferente — terminan con el mismo sonido (se pronuncian como si se escribieran igual al final): guy y pie, do y boo, throw y go, trees y breeze.

FIND the dog, moth, cat, flowers, mouse, and boy. Busca a: el perro, la polilla, el gato, las flores, el ratón, y el niño.

FREE online books: MulticulturalKidsBooks.com

I hear a noise,
SOUNDS in the house!

Escucho un ruido,
¡SONIDOS en la casa!

A squeak from the door,
steps on the floor,
a creak on the stair,

IT'S RAISING MY HAIR!

Un chirrido desde la puerta, pasos en el piso, un rechinar desde el escalón. ¡Los pelos se me levantan del temor!

El reloj hace tic tac.
Una polilla golpea contra
la ventana.

TICK
TICK
TICK
TICK
TICK

TAP
TAP

The clock ticks.
A moth taps my
window.

The water
heater goes,
TAT TAT TAT

El calentador
de agua dice:
TATO TATO

Piano sounds?
¿Son sonidos del piano?

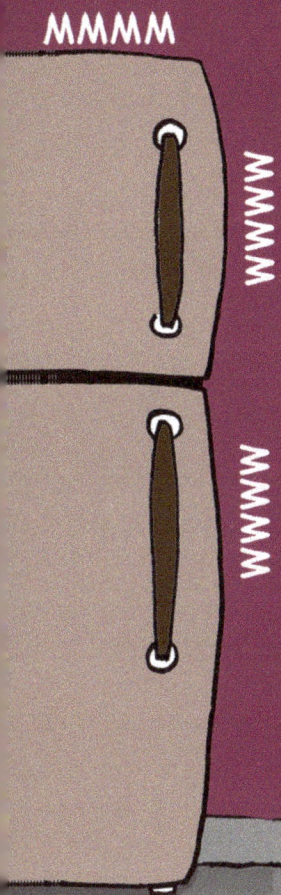

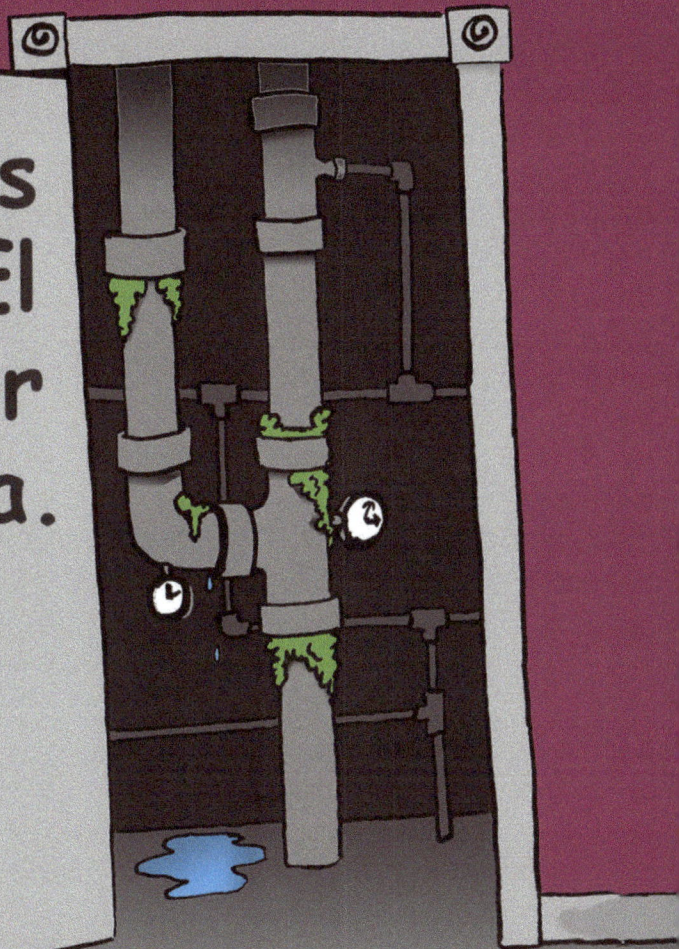

Trees creak in the breeze.

Los árboles rechinan en la brisa.

The furnace
roars to life

El calefactor
brama con vida

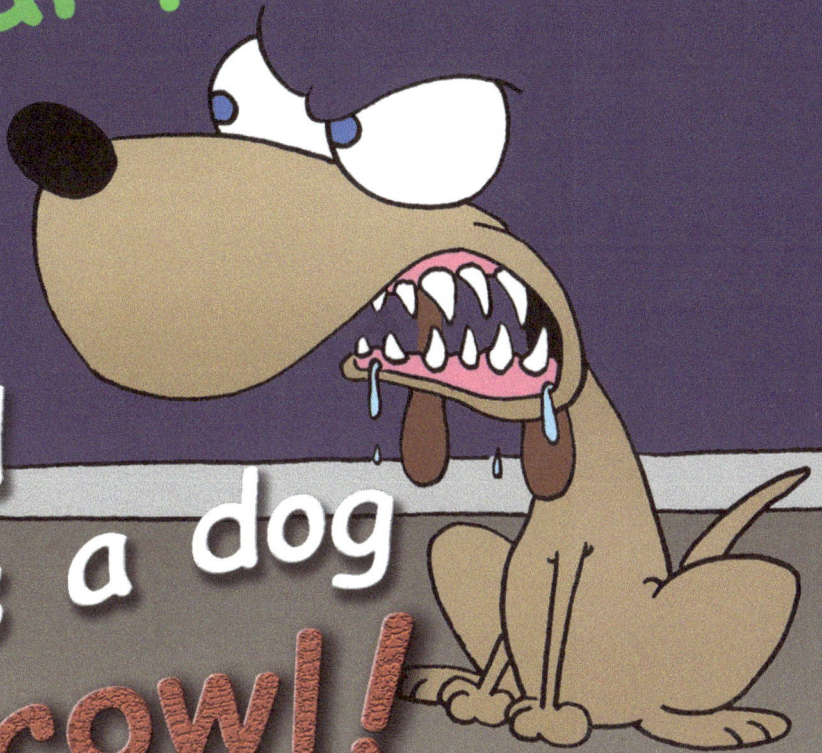

WUMP!

A DOOR SLAMS!

¡Una puerta se cierra de golpe!

¿Podría ser un duende o un fantasma, o un hombre malvado —que come perros en su pastel— podría estar en el corredor, o detrás de la pared, podría estar aquí **en la casa?**

Could it be that a goblin or ghost, or a really bad guy —who eats dogs in his pie— may be down the hall, or behind the wall, could be

here in our house?

O quizás sea un ratón.

Or, perhaps it's a mouse.

I think I know just what to do! I'll throw down the covers, and yell...

Yo creo saber exactamente qué hacer. Me quitaré las frazadas y gritaré:

fin

The End

Multicultural Books
by PREMIO PUBLISHING

YA & Middle Grade

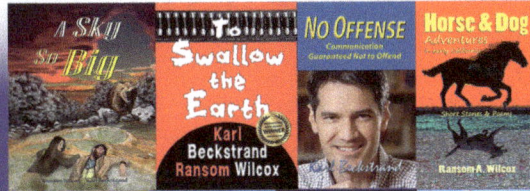

Spanish/bilingual

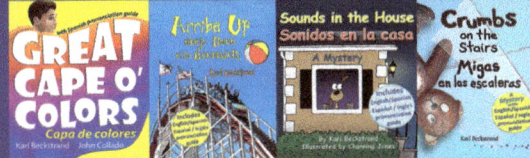

STEM

Food Books

Nonfiction

How-to

Mysteries

Wordless & Beginning reader

If you like our stories, please comment online.

www.ingramcontent.com/pod-product-compliance
Lightning Source LLC
Chambersburg PA
CBHW040253100426
42811CB00011B/1248